SIX QUESTIONS of AMERICAN

J

WHAT WAS THE CONTINENTAL CONGRESS?

And Other Questions about the Declaration of Independence

Candice Ransom

LERNER PUBLICATIONS · MINNEAPOLIS

A Word about Language

English word usage, spelling, grammar, and punctuation have changed over the centuries. We have preserved original spellings and word usage in the quotations included in this book.

Lerner Publications Company
A division of Lerner Publishing Group, Inc.
241 First Avenue North
Minneapolis, MN 55401 USA

For reading levels and more information, look up this title at www.lernerbooks.com.

Library of Congress Cataloging-in-Publication Data

Ransom, Candice F., 1952–
    What was the Continental Congress? : and other questions about the Declaration of Independence / by Candice Ransom.
       p.   cm. — (Six questions of American history)
    Includes bibliographical references and index.
    ISBN 978–0–7613–5227–3 (lib. bdg. : alk. paper)
    ISBN 978–0–7613–7239–4 (EB pdf)
    1. United States. Continental Congress—Juvenile literature. 2. United States. Declaration of Independence—Juvenile literature. 3. United States—Politics and government—1775–1783—Juvenile literature. I. Title.
E303.R357 2011
973.3'13—dc22   2010033371

Manufactured in the United States of America
2 – BR – 12/1/15

Main TABLE OF CONTENTS

THE SIX QUESTIONS HELP YOU DISCOVER THE FACTS!

INTRODUCTION

A man dressed in a black coat faced a group of serious men. The royal governor of the Virginia colony had forbidden the men to meet in Williamsburg, the capital. So they had gathered in St. John's Church in Richmond, Virginia.

It was March 23, 1775. The man in the black coat was Patrick Henry. He spoke out against King George III of Great Britain. Britain was heavily taxing the American colonies while giving colonists no voice in the British government. In 1768 British troops marched into Massachusetts to enforce new laws. These actions angered many colonists. Some spoke of going to war with Great Britain. But others wanted to make peace with the king.

Patrick Henry spread his arms wide and exclaimed, "Gentlemen may cry peace, peace, but there is no peace. The war is actually begun!" His dark eyes burned. "I know not what course others may take, but as for me, give me liberty, or give me death!"

Colonial leaders Richard Henry Lee and George Washington were in Henry's audience that night. They and other leaders such as Thomas Jefferson knew that colonists were unhappy. Something would have to be done.

Lee, Washington, and Jefferson would change the future of America. They would not do it alone. There were others like them. Who were these men?

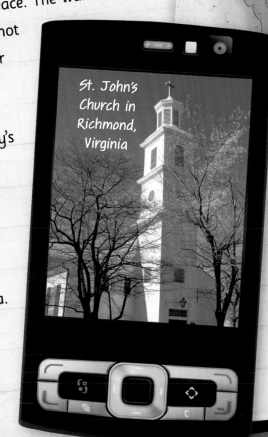

St. John's Church in Richmond, Virginia

THE AMERICAN COLONIES 1775

BRITISH TERRITORY

DISPUTED LAND

LAND CLAIMED BY SPAIN

ADDITIONAL LAND CLAIMED BY GREAT BRITAIN

THIRTEEN ORIGINAL COLONIES

NEW HAMPSHIRE

LEXINGTON

MASSACHUSETTS

NEW YORK

CONCORD

BOSTON

NEW YORK CITY

RHODE ISLAND

CONNECTICUT

PENNSYLVANIA

Philadelphia

NEW JERSEY

DELAWARE

MARYLAND

VIRGINIA

Richmond

Williamsburg

NORTH CAROLINA

SOUTH CAROLINA

GEORGIA

ATLANTIC OCEAN

In this 1848 hand-colored illustration, colonial leaders pray together before a meeting. These men would help decide the future of the American colonies.

5

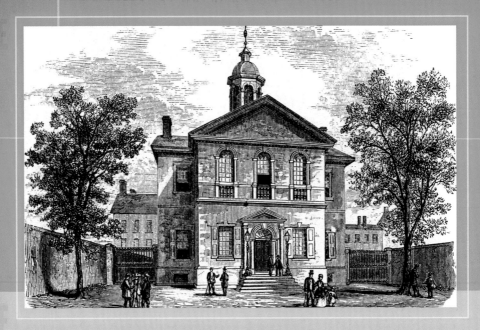

This is how Carpenters' Hall in Philadelphia, Pennsylvania, appeared in 1774.

ONE THE FIRST GATHERING

people given the power to act on behalf of other people at a meeting

On September 5, 1774, fifty-six delegates from twelve American colonies traveled to Philadelphia, Pennsylvania. Some rode hundreds of hot, dusty miles to reach the city. The delegates were all men, but they were from different backgrounds. There were Quakers from Pennsylvania, wealthy farmers from Virginia, and lawyers from New York. Only Georgia, the newest colony, did not send delegates.

members of a Christian group called the Religious Society of Friends

The delegates met at Carpenters' Hall on Chestnut Street. The men were nervous. They had never gathered before. They weren't sure what would happen at the meeting. But they came to help the colony of Massachusetts.

Most of the men were patriots. They believed that Great Britain had not treated American colonists fairly for many years. This led some patriots to believe in independence. They wanted the colonies to be free from British rule.

people with a strong sense of loyalty to their country. In colonial America, people who rebelled against British rule called themselves patriots.

Breaking away from Great Britain was a serious idea. The first American colony was founded by British settlers in 1607. More British settlers arrived, and the number of colonies grew. Each colony was ruled by a governor appointed by the British king. The colonies were tied to Great Britain by politics, trade, and tradition.

By the mid-1700s, more than two million people lived in the American colonies. The colonies still had royal governors. But each colony held its own assembly, or group of leaders who made and passed laws. Americans had grown used to freedom. And Great Britain had grown used to leaving its American colonies alone.

This portrait of Britain's King George III was painted by William Beechey (1783–1820).

the lawmaking part of the British government. Members of Parliament meet in London, England.

Then in 1765, Parliament issued the Stamp Act. The act charged American colonists a tax on newspapers and other printed documents. Great Britain needed money, and charging the colonies fees and taxes was an easy way to get it. The colonists disagreed. In Boston, Massachusetts, riots broke out over the Stamp Act.

people who speak or act for others

Americans had no representatives in Parliament, protesters said. Why should they pay the tax?

Parliament repealed, or did away with, the Stamp Act in 1766. But in 1767, British lawmakers passed the Townshend Acts. These laws charged Americans a tax on lead, paint, glass, paper, and tea. These things were produced in Great Britain. Taxes on them meant more money for British companies. The colonies fought back by boycotting

refusing to buy certain things or deal with certain people or organizations

British goods. King George sent British troops to try to put a stop to rebel activity.

In May 1773, Britain passed the Tea Act. That law tried to force colonists to buy tea from the British East India Company. American dockworkers refused to unload tea from British ships in Boston Harbor.

SONS OF LIBERTY

In 1765 a group of men met under an elm tree in Boston to protest the Stamp Act. They called themselves the Sons of Liberty. Patriots from all the colonies formed similar groups. Liberty Boys, Sons of Freedom, and Daughters of Liberty protested unfair tax laws. Leaders included Samuel Adams, Patrick Henry, John Adams, John Hancock, Charles Thomson, and Paul Revere. These patriots helped guide the colonies to independence.

During the Boston Tea Party in 1773, colonists dressed as Native Americans threw boxes of British tea into Boston Harbor. This 1846 color print shows the event happening in broad daylight. The real Boston Tea Party took place at night.

On the night of December 16, 1773, patriots led by Samuel Adams staged another protest against the Tea Act. They boarded three British ships docked in the harbor and dumped 342 chests of tea into the sea. The event became known as the Boston Tea Party.

In May 1774, more British troops led by General Thomas Gage arrived in Boston. British leaders closed Boston's port and banned town meetings. Trade was cut off. Boston—and all of Massachusetts—was in trouble.

In June the colonies decided to hold a general meeting in Philadelphia. They began planning the meeting and choosing delegates. In late August, citizens from towns in Suffolk County, Massachusetts, also met. They wrote a list of demands to Britain. The document was called the Suffolk Resolves.

In September 1774, delegates met at Carpenters' Hall. Virginia's delegates included Patrick Henry, Richard Henry Lee, and George Washington. Massachusetts delegates John Adams and his cousin Samuel Adams were there. Virginia delegate Peyton Randolph was elected president of the group. Charles Thomson from Philadelphia was chosen as secretary.

The group decided to call the meeting the Continental Congress. Next, the group decided how they would vote on issues. Each colony, no matter how large or small, would have one vote. The group thought that giving each colony equal power would help the delegates work together. "I am not a Virginian," Patrick Henry announced, "but an American." His words urged the delegates to unite.

For the next seven weeks, the members discussed a course of action. Outside the meeting, they shared meals and began to understand one another. John Adams wrote to his wife, Abigail, "There is in the Congress a collection of the greatest men upon this continent."

John Adams

"There is in the Congress a collection of the greatest men upon this continent."

As the Continental Congress began its work, the Massachusetts meeting finished its Suffolk Resolves. Massachusetts patriot Paul Revere rode on horseback from Massachusetts to Philadelphia. He delivered the resolves to Sam Adams.

The document stated that Americans would refuse to use British goods. They would create their own colonial governments. And each colony would form an army to defend itself. On September 17, the First Continental Congress accepted the resolves. John Adams was asked to write a declaration of rights. Colonists, Adams wrote, should have the same rights and freedoms enjoyed by all English subjects.

people governed by a monarch, such as a king or a queen

The document became known as the Declaration and Resolves of the First Continental Congress. The Congress sent the document to the British Parliament. If Britain accepted the declaration, the Congress would remain loyal to the king. But if Britain ignored America's complaints, the delegates would meet again in May 1775.

The meeting ended on October 26, 1774. Some delegates left believing that Britain would ignore the demands. They believed that war loomed ahead.

NEXT QUESTION

WHEN DID THE REVOLUTIONARY WAR BEGIN?

The British sent ships full of soldiers into Boston Harbor (below) in the 1760s and 1770s. The British hoped the soldiers would help end rebel activities. Instead, the acts angered many colonists.

A VIEW OF THE TOWN OF BOSTON WITH SEVERAL SHIPS OF WAR IN THE HARBOUR.

TWO WAR!

In the spring of 1775, the British government rejected the Declaration and Resolves of the First Continental Congress. Life in the colonies grew tense. The colonists divided into two groups. Patriots believed in independence from Britain. Loyalists remained loyal to the king. Both groups worried that there would be a war.

In Massachusetts, Sons of Liberty leader John Hancock helped form a special militia called the minutemen. Minutemen were soldiers who could be ready to fight on a moment's notice. The patriots stored guns for fifteen

militia: ordinary citizens who join together to fight as soldiers during an emergency

thousand minutemen in the town of Concord, about 20 miles (32 kilometers) west of Boston. British General Thomas Gage knew about the patriots' activities.

In Richmond, Virginia, Patrick Henry made his famous "give me liberty" speech on March 23, 1775. "If we wish to be free," he thundered, "we must fight!" The members at that meeting voted to train and arm Virginia's militia. Thomas Jefferson was one of the twelve men asked to prepare a plan to raise an army. Some Virginia soldiers wore badges on their shirts that said, "Liberty or Death."

"If we wish to be free, we must fight!"

A few weeks later, Massachusetts became the center of attention. The king had ordered General Gage to break up the rebels' committees and arrest the leaders. Gage was also ordered to destroy the storehouse of guns in Concord.

Patrick Henry

the crime of trying to overthrow one's own government

Sam Adams and John Hancock were the rebel leaders. If they were caught, they would be tried and possibly hanged for treason.

On April, 18, 1775, Hancock and Adams hid in Hancock's childhood home in the town of Lexington, about 5 miles (8 km) east of Concord. Patriot spies had warned Hancock and Adams that the British would leave Boston that night to find them. The spies said that Gage also planned to destroy the storehouse in Concord. But no one knew how the British were leaving Boston. Were they marching on land or rowing boats across the Charles River? Patriots set up a system of signals. If the British were coming by land, patriots would hang one lantern in the steeple of Boston's Old North Church. If the troops came by water, they would hang two lanterns. On the night of April 18, Paul Revere saw two lanterns go

This photo shows the house in Lexington, Massachusetts, where John Hancock and Sam Adams hid the night of April 18, 1775. The house was the home of Hancock's grandfather, also named John Hancock.

WHERE IS BOSTON?
Boston is in east central Massachusetts. To the east is Boston Harbor and the Atlantic Ocean. The Charles River runs north of downtown Boston.

up in the steeple. Revere rowed across the Charles River and jumped on a waiting horse. He rode through the countryside, warning people. Other patriots heard the alarm and jumped on their horses. They carried the message along to Lexington and Concord.

In Lexington, minutemen rushed out of their homes. Fathers, teenage sons, and grandfathers carried muskets, squirrel guns, and even hatchets. Eight hundred redcoats marched quickly up the road as the sun rose. Sixty or seventy minutemen faced them. The British major ordered the rebels to drop their guns. Then a shot rang out. No one knew which side had fired first.

British soldiers, so called because of their red uniforms

The British pointed their muskets at the colonists and fired. The colonists fought back, but they were outnumbered. When the shooting stopped, eight Americans lay dead.

The British marched on to Concord. The minutemen from that town met them on the North Bridge over the Concord River. The British shot and killed two minutemen. The Americans fired back. They killed three British soldiers and stormed over the bridge.

The redcoats ran back down the road toward Boston. The soldiers were surprised. They had thought the colonists' army would be nothing but farmers with sticks. They learned that the Americans had an organized force. British commander Sir Hugh Percy said, "Whoever dares to look at [the colonists] as a . . . mob will find himself much mistaken. They have men amongst them who know very well what they are about."

FIRST FIGHT

Colonists had clashed with British troops before Lexington and Concord. In 1767 Americans protested the Townshend Acts. Parliament did away with four of the five Townshend Acts. The tax on tea remained. British troops were posted in several colonial towns to stop further protests. Americans did not like this. On March 5, 1770, hundreds of colonists gathered at Boston's Custom House (a government building). They threw snowballs at eight British soldiers guarding the building. The soldiers were afraid of the angry crowd. They fired shots, and five Americans were killed. This event was called the Boston Massacre.

The soldiers were put on trial for murder. Patriot lawyer John Adams defended them. Adams did not want British troops in Boston. But he believed that the soldiers had a right to a fair trial.

British redcoats retreat from attacking minutemen. The colonial militia put up more of a fight than the British troops had expected.

Express riders carried news of the battles of Lexington and Concord. Even so, the southern colonies didn't hear about the fighting for two weeks. But when the colonies found out what had happened, they prepared for war. And the delegates began heading toward Philadelphia again to meet as the Second Continental Congress.

NEXT QUESTION

WHERE DID THE SECOND CONTINENTAL CONGRESS MEET?

Members of the Continental Congress met in the Assembly Room (below) of the Pennsylvania State House on May 10, 1775.

THREE CONGRESS MEETS AGAIN

John Adams returned to Philadelphia in May 1775. He noticed the city had changed. Colonial troops marched on the common. The city was preparing for war.

The Second Continental Congress gathered in the Pennsylvania State House, also on Chestnut Street. On May 10, Adams stepped into the assembly room for the first session.

Tall windows let in bright sunlight. The walls were painted white. Tables covered in green cloth stood between groups of chairs. The chairs were arranged in a half circle in front of a raised platform. The single chair on the platform had a sun carved into its high back.

Adams knew many of the men who had attended the First Continental Congress. Adams saw George Washington, wearing his scarlet and blue militia uniform. But there were some new faces too. John Hancock came with the Massachusetts group. Benjamin Franklin, the most famous American in the world, had just returned from London. He joined the meeting.

Once more, Georgia did not send representatives. The colony needed British troops to guard its western border against attacks by Native Americans. If Georgia sent delegates, Britain could pull out its troops and leave the colony defenseless.

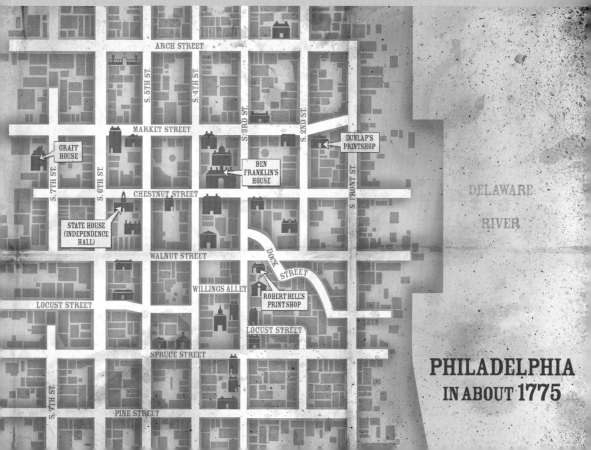

ARCH STREET

S. 5TH ST.
S. 4TH ST.
S. 3RD ST.
S. 2ND ST.

MARKET STREET

GRAFF HOUSE

DUNLAP'S PRINTSHOP

BEN FRANKLIN'S HOUSE

S. 7TH ST.
S. 6TH ST.
S. FRONT ST.

CHESTNUT STREET

DELAWARE RIVER

STATE HOUSE (INDEPENDENCE HALL)

WALNUT STREET

DOCK STREET

WILLINGS ALLEY

ROBERT BELL'S PRINTSHOP

LOCUST STREET

LOCUST STREET

SPRUCE STREET

S. 7TH ST.

PINE STREET

PHILADELPHIA
IN ABOUT 1775

Peyton Randolph was again elected president. Doors were locked, and windows were closed. Many British spies moved through Philadelphia. The meetings had to be kept secret.

Benjamin Franklin spoke for independence. Franklin told the delegates that King George III did not want peace. Many other delegates disagreed with Franklin. The colonies of New York, Pennsylvania, North Carolina, and South Carolina weren't ready to break away from Britain.

arguments between people (or groups) to decide issues

John Adams, too, believed independence was the only course. The endless debates and discussions filled him with frustration. But, he wrote to his wife, Abigail, "I will not [give up]."

When Peyton Randolph was called back to Virginia on state business, Thomas Jefferson was elected to replace him as a delegate. Jefferson set out from his home in Virginia, riding north to Philadelphia.

This print, published in 1876 by Currier and Ives, shows George Washington (center) accepting the position of commander of the Continental Army in 1775.

On June 14, 1775, Congress created an army to represent all the colonies. They called it the Continental Army. John Adams nominated George Washington as commanding general. Adams believed the colonies should call themselves the United Colonies.

Jefferson arrived for his first meeting in Congress on June 22. Soon after, he was appointed to a special committee. The committee was writing a document called a Declaration of the Causes and Necessity of Taking up Arms. Washington took a copy of the document to Massachusetts, where the Continental Army was gathering. He read the paper to his troops. The soldiers understood they were preparing to fight to protect their colonies.

WHY MEET IN PHILADELPHIA?

Philadelphia (shown above in 1776) was the largest, richest city in the colonies. Nearly thirty thousand people walked its neat, straight streets. Shipping was the city's main industry. Citizens could buy imported goods such as French wines and Chinese silks. The city's crafters also made furniture, watches, clocks, guns, nails, and glassware.

Philadelphia was a center for cultural and political activities. It had seven newspapers—more than London, the British capital, had. And since it was located in the middle of the colonies, Philadelphia was the perfect meeting place for the Continental Congress.

Still the delegates did not call for a formal separation from Britain. Pennsylvania's John Dickinson felt a peaceful agreement could be reached. He wrote a document called the Olive Branch Petition. (The branch from an olive tree is a symbol of peace.) The petition gave Britain one more chance to listen to America's complaints. John Adams thought Dickinson's document made the colonies look weak. But Congress agreed to send the petition.

Petition: a formal written request

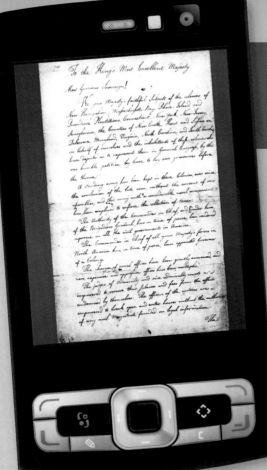

This is the first page of the Olive Branch Petition. It addresses King George as "the King's Most Excellent Majesty."

On July 20, delegates from Georgia arrived in Congress. Now all thirteen colonies belonged to the United Colonies.

William Penn, a former governor of Pennsylvania, sailed to England to deliver the Olive Branch Petition in person. He arrived in mid-August 1775. King George III rejected the petition. The king had decided that Britain and the colonies were enemies.

NEXT QUESTION

WHY DID THE CONTINENTAL CONGRESS CONTINUE TO MEET?

COMMON SENSE;

ADDRESSED TO THE

INHABITANTS

OF

AMERICA,

On the following interesting

SUBJECTS.

I. Of the Origin and Design of Government in general, with concise Remarks on the English Constitution.

II. Of Monarchy and Hereditary Succession.

III. Thoughts on the present State of American Affairs.

IV. Of the present Ability of America, with some miscellaneous Reflections.

Man knows no Master save creating HEAVEN,
Or those whom choice and common good ordain.
THOMSON.

Common Sense, written by Thomas Paine, was printed in 1776.

FOUR COLONIES TO STATES

Thomas Jefferson went home to Virginia in August 1775. Members in Congress often came and went. They left to take care of business or personal matters. Since each colony had only one vote, not all of a colony's delegates had to stay in Philadelphia.

Congress directed its attention to military matters. Washington's troops needed uniforms, guns, and food. Congress needed to figure out a way to get supplies to the Continental Army.

On January 10, 1776, Philadelphia printer Robert Bell published a pamphlet. The forty-seven-page booklet was

a short printed publication with a paper cover

called *Common Sense*. It was written by Thomas Paine, an Englishman who had recently moved to Philadelphia. Paine didn't use fancy words. His language could be understood by everyone.

Paine believed that the British system of a king (or queen) ruling over people was wrong. He felt America should be free. America should fight for its freedom. "The sun never shined on a cause of greater worth," he wrote. He ended the pamphlet with words printed in bold letters: "THE FREE AND INDEPENDENT STATES OF AMERICA."

People throughout the colonies read *Common Sense*. By February 1776, it had sold more than one hundred thousand copies. John Adams sent a copy to his wife, Abigail. Jefferson also read the pamphlet.

Paine's booklet gave colonists a new way to think about independence. They weren't arguing over taxes or rules from a distant king. They were fighting for freedom.

> "The sun never shined on a cause of greater worth."
>
> —Thomas Paine, writing about American independence in *Common Sense*

Thomas Paine

In response to the colonies' growing calls for independence, King George proclaimed that the colonists were traitors. They would be punished. He increased the size of the Royal Navy and ordered more troops to America. He even hired German soldiers to fight with the British Army.

On May 14, 1776, Jefferson returned to Philadelphia. Once again, he took his seat in Congress. The weather was as hot as midsummer.

Jefferson rented rooms in a new three-story brick house on Seventh and Market streets. The house had been built by a bricklayer named Jacob Graff. Jefferson rented the second floor—a bedroom and a parlor. A center hall let breezes pass through. The house was in a quiet neighborhood and was only a short walk to the Pennsylvania State House.

This print from the 1800s pictures the Graff house in Philadelphia. Thomas Jefferson lived here during the Continental Congress in 1776.

26

THOMAS JEFFERSON

Thomas Jefferson was born on April 12, 1743, in Virginia. He attended the College of William and Mary at the age of sixteen. Jefferson's interests included architecture, gardening, astronomy, and science. His Virginia home, Monticello (right), displays his inventions and collections. Jefferson became the third president of the United States in 1801. He died on July 4, 1826—the same day that John Adams died.

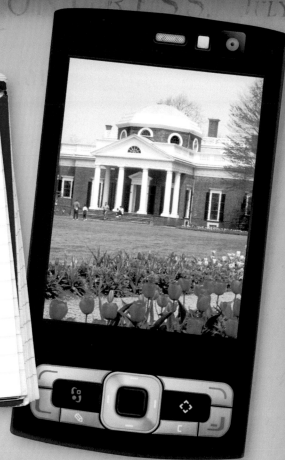

In Congress, delegates were calling the colonies states, using Paine's term. They ordered the states to form their own governments, separate from the colonial British rulers.

In Virginia, leaders gathered at a convention in Williamsburg to create a new state government. Jefferson longed to be there to help his fellow Virginians. He had several ideas for the new government. But Jefferson could not leave Philadelphia. Instead, he wrote a plan that included his ideas. He gave it to another Virginia delegate to Congress, George Wythe. Wythe was soon going home. Jefferson asked Wythe to deliver his plan to the Virginia Convention.

Jefferson's plan described a government where people could elect officials. His plan gave people religious freedom and freedom of the press. But the plan arrived too late. George Mason had already written the Virginia Declaration of Rights.

Near the end of May, the Virginia delegates in Philadelphia received a message from the Virginia Convention in Williamsburg. The message instructed the delegates to "declare the United Colonies free and independent states." For the first time, a colony officially announced that all the colonies should break away from Britain.

On Friday, June 7, 1776, Virginia delegate Richard Henry Lee stood to speak. His words rang out in the State House room. He said, "That these United Colonies are, and of right ought to be, free and independent States. . . ."

"These United Colonies are, and of right ought to be, free and independent States."

Richard Henry Lee

Congress chose Benjamin Franklin, Thomas Jefferson, Robert Livingston, John Adams, and Roger Sherman to write a statement explaining why America had to break away from Great Britain.

John Adams jumped up to second Lee's motion. The delegates began debating. New York, New Jersey, Pennsylvania, Delaware, Maryland, and South Carolina were against Lee's resolution. Finally, the delegates agreed to delay the vote for three weeks, until July 1.

motion. a formal plan of action at a meeting

If the vote passed, Congress decided, they would publish a formal declaration, or statement, of independence to explain why America was breaking away from Britain. On June 11, five men were appointed to the committee to write that declaration. They were John Adams, Benjamin Franklin, Robert Livingston of New York, Roger Sherman of Connecticut, and Thomas Jefferson. They were called the Committee of Five.

NEXT QUESTION

WHO DID THE COMMITTEE CHOOSE TO WRITE THE DECLARATION?

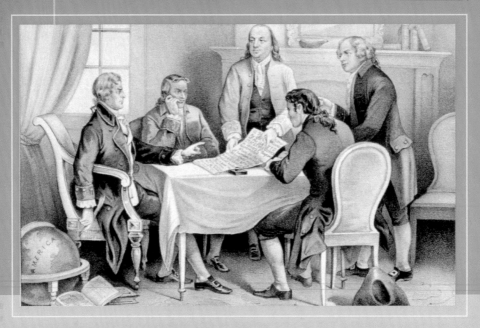

FIVE SEVENTEEN DAYS

The Committee of Five met at Benjamin Franklin's home. Franklin had been ill with gout, a painful disease of the joints. He hadn't been able to attend all the meetings in Congress. In his home, the committee members discussed what the declaration should say.

   Then they needed to decide who would write the document. No one is sure how Thomas Jefferson got the assignment. Benjamin Franklin was too ill to take on the project. And Roger Sherman and Robert Livingston weren't very good writers. Jefferson thought John Adams should write the declaration. At thirty-three, Jefferson felt he was too young. But Adams said no. He wanted Jefferson to write the document.

Adams had important reasons in choosing Jefferson. First, Adams knew he was too outspoken and unpopular in Congress. Second, Jefferson was a Virginian. As a group, Virginians were very popular and powerful in Congress. And third, Jefferson was the best writer in the group.

JOHN ADAMS

John Adams was born on October 30, 1735, in Massachusetts. He attended Harvard College when he was sixteen. He became a teacher and then a lawyer. In 1764 he married Abigail Smith. As a patriot, Adams opposed the Stamp Act. In 1776 he published a pamphlet called *Thoughts on Government*. Many of the new state governments used his ideas. Adams became the second U.S. president in 1797.

July 4, 1826, marked the fiftieth anniversary of the Declaration of Independence. John Adams died that day, not knowing that Thomas Jefferson had died just a few hours before.

Jefferson agreed to the task. He went back to his rented rooms in the Graff house. He rose at dawn each morning and read for a while. Then he soaked his feet in a basin of cold water. (He believed this practice would keep colds away.) Next, he played his violin softly. Breakfast was tea and biscuits.

After his morning routine, he was ready to work. He sat in a special chair in front of a portable writing desk. The mahogany desk was a rectangular box topped with a hinged writing board. The board could be placed in several positions.

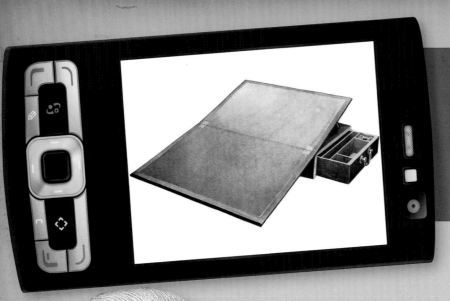

Thomas Jefferson

Underneath was a drawer for storing pens and paper. Jefferson had designed the chair and desk.

Dipping his pen in ink, Jefferson began writing. He hadn't brought books on government with him. But he remembered reading Thomas Paine's *Common Sense*. He recalled the Virginia Plan he had created only a few weeks before. He included some of the phrases from the plan in this new document.

Virginia's new constitution had been published in the *Pennsylvania Evening Post* on June 12. The author of the Declaration of Rights, George Mason, wrote that "all men are born equally free and independent. . . ." Jefferson thought about these ideas as he wrote.

the basic beliefs and laws of a nation, state, or group

When he got stuck, he paced the sitting room. Sometimes he walked down to the docks along the Delaware River and gazed at the ships. Other times he wandered into the countryside beyond Philadelphia.

Then he returned to his rooms in the Graff house and worked on the document. His pen flew over the paper. He rewrote paragraphs and sentences. When there were too many cross outs, Jefferson copied the draft on fresh paper.

This draft of the declaration shows Jefferson's handwriting and edits.

He still attended Congress every day, but his mind must have been on his project. For seventeen days, he wrote and revised. He ripped up messy drafts and wrote clean versions. When he was finished, he showed the document to the other committee members.

Roger Sherman read over the draft and gave his approval. Robert Livingston had returned home to New York, so he didn't see the draft. John Adams and Benjamin Franklin made a few changes.

American artist Jean Leon Gerome Ferris (1863–1930) made this print showing Jefferson standing as Franklin and Adams (left and middle) read his draft of the Declaration of Independence.

On Friday, June 28, Jefferson delivered a fresh copy to Congress. The document was read aloud by Charles Thomson, the secretary. Then Congress ended for the day. It would meet again on Monday, July 1. On that day, the delegates would vote for or against independence.

WHAT HAPPENED TO JEFFERSON'S DRAFTS?

Jefferson tore up drafts and copied the Declaration of Independence over several times. One draft was written between June 11 and June 21, 1776. That was given to John Adams and Benjamin Franklin for comments. After that, Jefferson wrote another draft, revising nearly one-third of the document. This version includes changes made by Adams and Franklin. This draft can be found in the Manuscript Division of the Library of Congress, in Washington, D.C. A scrap of one of Jefferson's early drafts can also be found in the Library of Congress.

NEXT QUESTION

WHY WAS THE DECLARATION OF INDEPENDENCE CREATED?

SIX INDEPENDENCE AT LAST

The afternoon of July 1, 1776, was steamy hot. The windows in the State House were open a few inches to let in air. The opened windows also let in horseflies that bit the delegates' legs through their thick stockings. Outside, the sky grew dark with the threat of a storm.

The men had been sitting since nine o'clock that morning. At last it was time to discuss Richard Henry Lee's resolution. Should the colonies become free and independent states? John Dickinson of Pennsylvania stood to speak.

Independence, he said, would mean an all-out war. Where would the colonies get the money to feed and clothe an army? If they broke away from Britain before they were ready, it would be the same as destroying a house in winter before building a new one. Suppose, Dickinson went on, that the war dragged on. Britain could lose so much money, the king would give up. Then America's old enemies, France and Spain, might take over the colonies. And which European countries would trade with a group of rebel colonies? More important, America had no central government. Congress could be broken up at any time. How would the colonies be governed?

Thunder crashed and lightning flashed when John Adams rose to respond. No one recorded his words, but Adams described the new nation they would create. Jefferson recalled later that Adams's speech "moved us from our seats." The colonies were already at war. They must fight, and they must win.

A close-up of Trumbull's painting reveals thoughtful faces as the delegates listen to the declaration. Many knew the next step could mean war with Great Britain.

A vote was taken. Pennsylvania and South Carolina voted against independence. New York had no instructions from its state government on how to vote. Delaware didn't have enough delegates—Caesar Rodney had gone home. A messenger was sent to bring him back. Congress postponed the vote until the next day.

On the morning of July 2, rain slashed against the closed windows. The delegates were on edge. John Dickinson and Robert Morris, both from Pennsylvania, weren't there. And where was Rodney?

They could wait no longer. Charles Thomson called for a vote. New Hampshire, Massachusetts, Connecticut, and Rhode Island voted for independence. Once more New York stated that it could not vote. John Dickinson and Robert Morris did not want to vote for independence, so they stayed away from the meeting. Without them, New Jersey and Pennsylvania voted yes. Suddenly, the door burst open, and Caesar Rodney rushed in. He had ridden 80 miles (129 km) in pouring rain without stopping. Delaware voted yes, along with Virginia, North Carolina, South Carolina, and Georgia.

Caesar Rodney

The delegates realized the colonies had just become the United States of America. There was no turning back. They planned to discuss Thomas Jefferson's document the next day.

July 3 was cool and clear. In the State House, Thomson read Jefferson's document aloud. The delegates began making comments for changes. The whole world would read this document. Other countries—as well as American citizens—needed to know the reasons why the United States broke away from Britain. People needed to know that King George III had forced taxes on Americans and was waging war against them. Word by word, line by line, the delegates discussed the document. Jefferson listened but didn't speak.

The next day, July 4, Congress continued its work on the declaration. When they were finished, the document had simpler language. John Hancock signed the document.

Charles Thomson added his signature as a witness. The four-page handwritten document was sent to John Dunlap, a printer on Market Street. Dunlap printed two hundred copies of the broadside. On Saturday, July 6, the Declaration of Independence was printed in the *Pennsylvania Evening Post*.

Fast riders carried copies of Dunlap's broadside to cities and villages from New Hampshire to Georgia. Bonfires blazed and church bells rang as people celebrated. In New York City, the Continental Army heard the Declaration of Independence on July 9. People tore down a statue of George III on one of the city's main streets. The lead in the statue was later melted into bullets for the army.

broadside: a sheet of paper printed on only one side

WHAT IS THE LIBERTY BELL?

In 1753 workers lifted a bell into the steeple of the Pennsylvania State House. The bell weighed 2,080 pounds (943 kilograms) and was made of copper and other metals. It bore the words, "Proclaim Liberty throughout all the land unto all the inhabitants thereof." The Liberty Bell rang to call lawmakers to meetings of the Philadelphia Assembly and to alert citizens to important announcements.

On July 8, 1776, bells—including the Liberty Bell—rang out across Philadelphia. The bells announced that the Declaration of Independence would be read in public for the first time.

Sometime in the early to mid 1800s, a crack in the side of the Liberty Bell widened. The crack silenced the bell. The bell remains a symbol of colonial America's fight for independence.

WHERE IS THE LIBERTY BELL?

Since 2003 the bell has hung in the Liberty Bell Center—part of Independence National Historic Park in Philadelphia.

President's House Site — Market Street
Liberty Bell Center
5th Street
Chestnut Street
Independence Hall
6th Street
Walnut Street
Independence Square
Philadelphia
GPS

The official copy of the Declaration of Independence was handwritten on a large sheet of parchment by Timothy Matlack. It was titled, "The Unanimous Declaration of the Thirteen United States of America." On August 2, 1776, the delegates who were present gathered to sign the parchment. John Hancock wrote his signature in large, fancy letters. Eventually, fifty-six delegates signed the Declaration of Independence. Thomas McKean of Delaware was the last to sign. His signature appeared in 1777, or possibly as late as 1781.

agreed to by all

The signers knew they were committing treason. If America lost the war with Britain, the delegates could be hanged. But they believed in freedom. George Washington's troops fought the British from 1775 to 1781. In October 1781, British general Charles Cornwallis surrendered to Washington at Yorktown, Virginia. In 1783 the Treaty of Paris officially ended the war and announced to the world the new country of the United States of America.

NEXT QUESTION

HOW DO WE KNOW WHAT HAPPENED AT THE SECOND CONTINENTAL CONGRESS?

Primary Source: A Letter from John Adams

The best way to learn about any historical event is with primary sources. Primary sources are created near the time being studied. They include diaries or journals, letters, newspaper articles, documents, speeches, pamphlets, photos, paintings, and other items. They are made by people who have firsthand knowledge of the event.

Secretary Charles Thomson noted the delegates' daily attendance at the Second Continental Congress. But he didn't record details of debates. Thomas Jefferson also kept a record of the meetings from June 7 to August 1, 1776. But Jefferson's notes were not daily accounts.

John Adams is one of the best sources for information about the Second Continental Congress. Adams kept a journal and copies of his letters to make sure he'd have a record of, as he said later, "the great events which are passed, and those which are rapidly advancing."

In 1822 Timothy Pickering, a former U.S. secretary of state, wrote to John Adams. Pickering wanted to know how the Declaration of Independence had come to be written. Adams was eighty-seven years old when he answered Pickering's question. He described an event that had taken place more than forty years before:

> The committee met, discussed the subject, and then appointed Mr. Jefferson and me to make the draught [draft], I suppose because we were the two first on the list . . . [When] Jefferson proposed to me to make the draught I said, "I will not." . . . [Jefferson asked,] "Why will you not?" [I said,] "Reason first—You are a Virginian, and a Virginian ought to appear at the head of this business. Reason second—I am obnoxious, suspected, and unpopular. You are much otherwise. Reason third—You can write ten times better than I can."
>
> "Well," said Jefferson, "if you are decided, I will do as well as I can."

TELL YOUR CONTINENTAL CONGRESS STORY

Imagine you are a delegate from one of the thirteen colonies that attended the Second Constitutional Convention in the spring and summer of 1776. You keep a daily diary. Write several entries about your experience as a delegate.

WHAT colony are you from?

WHAT do you do for a living?

HOW did you travel to Philadelphia?

HOW do you feel about independence from Great Britain? Are you for or against it?

WHAT would you do if British troops invaded your colony?

WHAT do you hope will happen at the convention?

WHO among the other delegates do you most admire? Why?

USE **WHO, WHAT, WHERE WHY, WHEN,** AND **HOW** TO THINK OF OTHER QUESTIONS TO HELP YOU CREATE YOUR STORY!

Timeline

1607

English settlers found the first American colony in Jamestown, Virginia.

1765

The British Parliament passes the Stamp Act, a tax on printed materials.

1766

Parliament repeals the Stamp Act.

1767

The Townshend Acts tax tea, lead, paint, glass, and paper imported from Great Britain.

1768

British troops arrive in Boston to enforce unpopular new laws.

1770

On March 5, five colonists are shot by British redcoats near the Boston Custom House. Patriots call the event the Boston Massacre.

In April four of the five Townshend Acts are repealed.

1773

On May 10, Britain passes the Tea Act.

On December 16, colonists stage the **Boston Tea Party** protest, dumping 342 chests of British tea into Boston Harbor.

1774

Parliament closes Boston's port to punish the city for its protests.

The First Continental Congress meets in Philadelphia. It sends its Declaration and Resolves to Parliament.

1775

Parliament rejects the Declaration and Resolves of the First Continental Congress.

On May 10, the Second Continental Congress meets in Philadelphia.

In June Congress appoints **George Washington** commander of the Continental Army.

The Revolutionary War begins with the battles of Lexington and Concord.

1776

Thomas Paine's *Common Sense* is published.

Thomas Jefferson writes the Declaration of Independence.

On July 4, Congress adopts the Declaration of Independence.

On July 8, the Liberty Bell is rung in Philadelphia and the **Declaration of Independence is read in public** for the first time.

On August 2, delegates who are present in Congress sign the Declaration of Independence.

Source Notes

4   Russell Freedman, *Give Me Liberty! The Story of the Declaration of Independence* (New York: Holiday, 2000), 30.

10 Natalie S. Bober, *Countdown to Independence: A Revolution of Ideas in England and Her American Colonies: 1760–1776* (New York: Simon & Schuster, 2001), 223.

10 Ibid., 225.

10 Ibid.

13 Ibid., 241.

13 Ibid.

16 Freedman, 43.

20 David McCullough, *John Adams* (New York, Simon & Schuster, 2001), 88.

25 Bober, 303.

25 Ibid.

28 McCullough, 117.

28 Freedman, 61.

28 Ibid.

33 McCullough, 121.

37 Ibid., 127.

42 Joseph J. Ellis, *American Creation: Triumphs and Tragedies at the Founding of the Republic* (New York: Knopf, 2007), 6.

42 Ashbrook Center for Public Affairs, "John Adams to Timothy Pickering, August 6, 1822," Teaching American History, 2008, http://teachingamericanhistory.org/library/index.asp?document=2081 (September 21, 2010).

Selected Bibliography

Ashbrook Center for Public Affairs. "John Adams to Timothy Pickering, August 6, 1822." Teaching American History. 2008. http://teachingamericanhistory.org/library/index.asp?document=2081 (September 21, 2010).

Bober, Natalie S. *Countdown to Independence: A Revolution of Ideas in England and Her American Colonies: 1760–1776*. New York: Simon & Schuster, 2001.

Ellis, Joseph J. *American Creation: Triumphs and Tragedies at the Founding of the Republic*. New York: Knopf, 2007.

Freedman, Russell. *Give Me Liberty! The Story of the Declaration of Independence*. New York: Holiday, 2000.

Lancaster, Bruce. *The American Heritage History of the American Revolution*. New York: American Heritage Books, 1971.

McCullough, David. *John Adams*. New York, Simon & Schuster, 2001.

Further Reading and Websites

Declaration of Independence
http://www.nara.gov/historical-docs/
This site shows pictures of the original document and gives interesting facts about how it is being preserved. You can "sign" and print a copy of the document.

Fink, Sam. *Declaration of Independence*. New York: Scholastic, 2007. The famous document is broken up into hand-lettered phrases for easier understanding. Humorous art illustrates high-flown ideas with down-to-earth pictures. Back matter includes a timeline and a glossary.

Fradin, Dennis Brindell. *The Signers: The 56 Stories behind the Declaration of Independence*. New York: Walker, 2003. Organized by colonies, this book gives brief histories of the lives of the men who signed the Declaration of Independence. Facts are also presented in maps, charts, and period-style illustrations.

Freedman, Russell. *Give Me Liberty! The Story of the Declaration of Independence*. New York: Holiday House, 2000.

Gondosch, Linda. *How Did Tea and Taxes Spark a Revolution?* Minneapolis: Lerner Publications Company, 2011. Read about the daring Boston Tea Party and other protests that pushed the American colonies to declare independence from Great Britain.

Masoff, Joy. *Chronicle of America: American Revolution, 1700–1800*. New York: Scholastic, 2000. This book describes life in the colonies, the causes that led to the American Revolution, and the war. Fun bits of information are included, such as recipes and colonial games.

McPherson, Stephanie Sammartino. *Liberty or Death: A Story about Patrick Henry*. Minneapolis: Millbrook Press, 2003. Patrick Henry was a lawyer, a farmer, a business owner, and a passionate patriot. Learn his life story, from his boyhood in Virginia to his role as a fiery revolutionary leader.

Ransom, Candice. *Who Wrote the U.S. Constitution?* Minneapolis: Lerner Publications Company, 2011. Eleven years after the Declaration of Independence, many of the same people gathered again in Philadelphia to write a set of rules to guide the new nation. Read the exciting story behind the U.S. Constitution.

St. George, Judith. *The Journey of the One and Only Declaration of Independence*. New York: Philomel, 2005. This fact-packed book describes the lively travels of the Declaration of Independence after its signing, during the Revolutionary War, the War of 1812, and other wars, as well as the ways it was transported and the many places it was hidden.

Index

Photo Acknowledgments

The images in this book are used with the permission of: © iStockphoto.com/DNY59, p. 1; National
Archives, pp. 1 (background) and all Declaration of Independence backgrounds; © iStockphoto.com/
sx70, pp. 3 (top), 8, 16, 22 (bottom), 27 (left), 31, 35 (top), 40 (left); © iStockphoto.com/Ayse Nazli
Deliormanli, pp. 3 (bottom), 43 (bottom left); © iStockphoto.com/Serdar Yagci, pp. 4-5 (background), 43
(background); © iStockphoto.com/Andrey Pustovoy, pp. 4, 14, 23 (top), 27 (right), 32 (top); © James
Schwabel/Alamy, p. 4 (inset); © Bill Hauser & Laura Westlund/Independent Picture Service, pp. 4-5,
19; The Granger Collection, New York, pp. 5, 21, 26, 45 (top); The Art Archive, p. 6; © Image Asset
Management Ltd./SuperStock, p. 7; Library of Congress, pp. 9 (LC-USZC4-523), 30 (LC-USZC2-2243),
34 (LC-USZC4-9904), 38 (LC-USZC4-2969), 44 (LC-USZC4-523); © National Portrait Gallery/Snark
Archives © Photo12/The Image Works, p. 10; © North Wind Picture Archives, pp. 12, 17 (top), 22 (top),
27 (inset), 28, 29 (top), 32 (inset), 33, 45 (bottom); © Stock Montage/Archive Photos/Getty Images, pp.
12-13, 32 (bottom); © Brian Jannsen/Alamy, p. 14 (inset); © Bettmann/CORBIS, pp. 15 (top), 20;
© Laura Westlund/Independent Picture Service, pp. 15 (inset), 40 (inset); © iStockphoto.com/Talshiar,
pp. 15 (bottom), 40 (right); © Joe Sohm/The Image Works, p. 18; © MPI/Archive Photos/Getty Images,
pp. 23 (inset), 24; © The Huntington Library, Art Collections & Botanical Gardens/The Bridgeman
Art Library, p. 25; © SuperStock/SuperStock, pp. 36, 43 (bottom right); © Boltin Picture Library/The
Bridgeman Art Library, p. 37; Private Collection/Peter Newark American Pictures/The Bridgeman Art
Library, p. 41 (top).

Front cover: © SuperStock/SuperStock. Back cover: National Archives.